THE GOAL OF JAPANESE EXPANSION

THE AUTHOR

THE GOAL
OF
JAPANESE EXPANSION

BY

TATSUO KAWAI

TOKYO

THE HOKUSEIDO PRESS

1938

PREFACE

JAPAN is a growing nation. She has grown in population, in culture and in industry and commerce at an astonishing tempo within the past few decades. And she is still growing.

An examination of the spiritual and historic backgrounds of the Japanese race will reveal the secret of its apparently sudden and phenomenal progress. In brief, this progress is a manifestation of the cosmic force which unites divergent elements, generates life, and fosters growth, and which the Japanese call "Musubi."

Japanese expansion on the Asiatic continent is an inevitable development of history. But Japan desires neither conquest nor territory. Musubi is not merely a biological force, but it is a spiritual power that chastens, and beautifies, admitting of no sordid elements of selfishness. The Japanese ideal of "the world, one household," as was enunciated by the Emperor Jimmu, carries no thought of domination, but envisages universal concord on the basis of freedom and equality. Japan's objective in her gigantic campaign in China to-day is to bring about through the elimination of the forces of destruction a new unity and solidarity for the family of Oriental nations — an Oriental system which is based on the philosophy of Musubi, and which will insure peace and security for East Asia.

The China Affair, stupendous tragedy as it is in itself, must be regarded as a necessary step toward the creation of a new era for the Orient. And therein lies the goal of Japanese expansion.

Such is the thesis of the book, " Hatten Nippon no Mokuhyo," which was written last spring with a view to elucidating the spiritual background of the Japanese campaign in China. The translator has taken the liberty of re-arranging certain chapters and omitting many classical allusions and quotations, both Japanese and Chinese. The English version is, therefore, somewhat altered in form and greatly reduced in size as compared with the original; and moreover, it is shorn mostly of the literary merits which distinguish Mr. Kawai's writing. However, it is hoped that the present book will serve to convey the author's conviction and faith — which is also our nation's conviction and faith—regarding Japan's mission in East Asia and in the world.

THE TRANSLATOR

December, 1938.

CONTENTS

CHAPTER I

EXPANSION OF THE JAPANESE RACE

1. MORALITY OF RACIAL EXPANSION

An American author, Mr. Walter Thompson, wrote in 1929 that the population of Japan presented a grave world problem. Whether or not the Japanese could be provided with an outlet for their surplus population is a question, he argued, of whether there should be war or not. Pointing out the fact that the decisive factor in Sino-Japanese relations was Japan's economic interests in Manchuria, he said that if China should ignore the vested interests of Japan, it would perhaps lead to a war between the two countries. In the next two or three decades Japan would be very likely compelled to seek natural resources abroad. With the increase of population, an ever growing economic pressure would be felt by the workers. Thus the acquisition of new territories by Japan would not be the demand of any particular class, but rather a national necessity, and the movement

9

for territorial expansion would have the support of
the entire nation.   The directions of this movement were already set.   As regards North America,
the door had long been closed.   South America,
especially Brazil, offered an outlet, but it was doubt-
ful whether there were possibilities for Japanese
emigration in this direction to a degree sufficient
to solve Japan's population problem.   Siberia was
too cold.   Consequently the only natural direction for Japanese advance lay in the West and in
the South.   Such were the views of this American
author.

In fact, Japan has expanded phenomenally not
only in population but in all other phases of her
national life.   As was predicted by Mr. Thompson, the Manchurian Incident occurred in 1931
because China had ignored our vested interests in
Manchuria—indeed, ignored thereby Japan's fundamental right to national existence.

The Manchurian Incident marked the beginning of extraordinary military preparations by the
Soviet Union along its Far Eastern frontier.   Find-
ing in Russia a convenient check upon Japan, the
Kuomintang Government launched its anti-Japanese campaign on a nation-wide scale.   In the

meantime, thanks to Japan's policy of justice and
equity, Manchuria became an independent State—
heralding a new Asiatic unity. Strange are the
ways of history. Jealous Powers tried to intervene
in the Sino-Japanese imbroglio by invoking action on the part of the League of Nations, only to
expose before the world the helplessness of that
organization. The collapse of the League was fol-
lowed by the rise of Germany and Italy, as sudden
as it was significant.

In October, 1933, Fuehrer Hitler declared :
" Germany has too many people for her territory.
To deprive a great nation of its necessary livelihood
is after all against the interest of the world. We
believe we have the same ability as other nations
in the matter of the control and administration of
colonies." Signor Mussolini in his address to the
Fascist Congress in March, 1934, said as follows :
" Our mission is dictated by history and by the
facts of geography. Italy, of all European Powers,
lies closest to Asia and Africa. We have no territorial ambitions, but we desire to achieve a natural
expansion which promises close co-operation between Italians and the peoples of Africa and the
Orient. I warn those nations that are already satis-

fied, and those that have already arrived at their goal, not to obstruct Italy's path of spiritual development and economic expansion." Once more as in the days before the Great War, colonies have become the bone of political contention in Europe.

The "haves" and the "have-nots" are familiar terms in a discussion of the question of colonial redistribution.   As a matter of fact, it is easier to understand the dynamic character of the conflict if we view it as one between the "grown" and the "growing." There are countries that may be classified under the " have-nots," such as Switzerland or Norway, which are scarcely interested in colonial questions, while among those who "have" there remains the question of degree.   Besides, between possession and non-possession there is a merely static contrast, which does not necessarily involve either a struggle to alter the *status quo* of mutual relations, or any question of morality.   It may, therefore, be said that the characteristic of 20th century international politics is the dynamic opposition and strife between the nations that have fully grown and those that are still growing.   The ethics of human society should not condemn the positive expansion of the growing nations.   An

economic system based upon freedom of trade has
been replaced by a system of tariffs and embargoes,
which hinders the movement of raw materials, op-
pressing intolerably those nations like Japan, Germany and Italy, which have not sufficient natural
resources at their disposal, and rendering it impossible for them to maintain their existence as growing nations.   Friction and conflict are bound to
arise from economic dislocation of such a serious
character.

It is significant that leaders in the "grown"
nations, such as Snowden in England and Sarraux
in France, should echo the words of Hitler and
Mussolini and call for the redistribution of colonies.

In September, 1935, "Liberty," an American
magazine, published an article by the late Colonel
House, in which he declared that "the haves are
equally responsible as are the have-nots for having plunged the world into this critical condition.
Great Britain should be held to blame no less than
Italy which has started war in Africa, or Germany
sowing seeds of disquiet in Europe."   To sleep
on one's rights means generally the loss of those
rights.   The right of ownership, regardless of how
perfectly it is established upon a legal basis, is not

morally tenable unless the property owned is administered properly and devoted to a useful end. To sleep on one's property right, without using or administering it properly, is an unpardonable crime from the standpoint of community interest and social morality. This applies to individual nations as well as to individual men.

Hitler had good reason for telling the world that Germany "has the same ability as other nations to control and administer colonies." Germany was fully justified in throwing off the yoke of the League of Nations, since some of her lost colonies could have been exploited more fully by the gifted German people for the benefit of the whole world than by their present owners. Nations with rapidly growing populations and inadequate resources have a far more legitimate claim to the world's remaining unexploited areas than those nations which already enjoy the blessings of abundance. The struggle of nations to overcome their material deficiencies by acquiring extra territory is sometimes called imperialism. In the case of Japan, however, this term is not entirely applicable, because the process of Japanese expansion is not the same as that in the West. In the first

place, Japan does not desire to incorporate extra
territory into her Empire in the form of new colonies or dependencies.   But of even greater importance is the fact that Japan's so-called "imperial"
relations with the Asiatic mainland have involved
significant spiritual and cultural aspects which have
been completely lacking in the more mundane imperialism of the West.

Asia's spiritual civilization blossomed forth
first in India and in China.   Japan, through her
2000-year contact with China, transplanted the
best of Chinese culture onto her own soil, which,
when imbued with the spirit of Japan, resulted in
the birth of the Asiatic spirit.   Though she came
in contact with Occidental civilization long after
China, Japan preceded her neighbour in adopting
and adapting the institutions and systems of Europe.
Thus upon Japan's realization of the importance
and sanctity of the worldly life of man, a new road
was opened for the progress of Asia.

According to Asiatic philosophy, man's ulti-
mate aim is to enter Nirvana—in which the individual soul is fused completely with the cosmic
soul.   It teaches the negation of one's self in order
to find a greater self.   Outwardly Japan's expan-

sion is a normal phenomenon.   But there is idealism behind this expansion, and its results are totally
different in character from those achieved by mere
aggression or conquest.   What burdens, financial
and otherwise, Japan has borne through the annexation of Chosen!   What restraints and self-denials
have been imposed upon Japanese capitalists and
workmen in order to maintain the independence
of Manchoukuo!   Expansion means to Japan the
multiplication of obligations and sacrifice.   That
is because Japan, under the discipline of Asiatic
idealism, does not desire to prosper at the expense
of the rest of humanity, but she seeks to find in
the common prosperity of the whole of Asia her
own happiness and well-being.

Japan's expansion and progress will render
possible the liberation of China from what Sun Yat-
sen called a "quasi-colonial status," enabling her
to stand with Japan on a footing of equality and reciprocity as a free and sovereign State in the Asiatic
system.   Japan does not wish to conquer China or
any other country.   She is striving to bring about
such conditions as will make it possible for Asiatic
nations to unite in one Asiatic system and live an
Asiatic life through mutual helpfulness.

The perfect State was called Tatung (great oneness) by the ancients in China, and Daiwa (great
harmony) by the Japanese, both pointing to the
same ideal embodied in the motto, "The world,
one household." The practice of universal brotherhood is indeed the moral purpose of Oriental imperialism.

In the following chapters it is proposed to de-
scribe the growth of the Japanese population, the
various stages of national expansion and the spiritual
and material aspects of the newly-created Japanese
civilization; to examine how the different cultures
of Asia have been absorbed and assimilated by
Japan; then to retrace the history of her continental expansion; and finally, to dwell briefly on
the significance of the present China Affair in history and explain the inevitable rise of the movement for Japan-Manchoukuo-China unification
within an Asiatic system.

2. INCREASE OF THE POPULATION

Japan's progress in every field of human activity—in industry and commerce and in science
and arts—has been as rapid and steady as the growth
of her population. The population of Japan proper

increased from 33,110,000 in 1872 to 61,380,000 in 1913. According to the last census, taken in 1935, the figure had further increased to 69,250,-000. If the people of Chosen and of those living in the colonies are added, the population is equal to one-twentieth of the total population of the world or one-eleventh of that of Asia.

The Japanese race with this astonishing fecundity is endowed at the same time with a sturdy body, clear intelligence, courage and adaptability. It is easy to visualize the picture of a youthful and adventuresome Japan from the following statistical table showing the age composition of her population.

AGE COMPOSITION OF JAPANESE POPULATION

Year	0-14 Years	%	15-59 Years	%	60-99 Years	%
1925	21,924	36.70	33,223	55.62	4,589	7.68
1930	22,301	35.40	35,964	57.06	4,731	7.51
1935	23,471	35.10	38,374	57.40	5,014	7.50

* Unit 1,000

The original home of this young Japan is the Japanese archipelago—a string of small islands, to which have been added, as a result of the Sino-Japanese and Russo-Japanese Wars, Formosa, Chosen and South Saghalien, territories altogether equal

in area to four-fifths of Japan proper. Japan is
thus made up of pieces of land varying widely in
climatic and social conditions, which, however,
have been organically welded into an empire by
an efficient and rational system of administration.

While the classic doctrine that economic possibilities constitute a postulate of population increase
is sound, the fact should not be overlooked that
an increase of population is a powerful stimulant
to economic development. There is a functional
relationship between the population and the economy of a country. And in the case of Japan, her
economic development is attributable to the fecundity of the race more than to any other factor.

The peculiarity of Japanese economic life lies
in the density, concentration, and rapid growth of
the population. The well-nigh seventy million
people of Japan proper are crowded together at the
rate of 169 per square-kilometre. Coming after
Belgium with 270, Holland with 233 and England
with 188, Japan stands fourth in the world in density of population. If, however, we exclude un-
inhabitable mountainous regions and compute the
populations of these countries on the basis of arable
land alone, Japan's density is 1000 per square-kilo-

metre, which is the highest figure in the world, surpassing easily that of 800 for Holland. Moreover, the larger portion of this immense number is concentrated in but a few localities.

Even now the Japanese population is increasing at the rate of about one million a year. The nation, conquering that poverty which necessarily attends a rapid population growth, has been promoting its welfare and happiness by ceaseless and tireless labour.

The harmony between quality and quantity— "between intellectual development and numerical increases, physical fitness and the age composition, the creative energy and the population factors that render it possible "—the mysterious harmony of all these elements finds a living example in the Japanese race. The one hundred million Japanese now so active in the world have, however, passed through a long period of quiet preparation. In that period the people amalgamated with their native cult of Shinto the philosophies and religions of China and India, and produced an efflorescence of Oriental culture on their soil. East Asia had long become a distinct cultural region under Japanese leadership. Then, since the Meiji Restoration

Japan, by importing Occidental civilization and achieving socially and economically a phenomenal advance, has emerged as the pioneer of a new order and civilization, while politically she has assumed the rôle of the major stabilizing force of East Asia.

While scholars here and there, after a superficial examination of the phenomenon of Japanese expansion, were discussing apprehensively "danger spots in world population " or " population pressure in the Far East," the mighty power of one hundred million people made Japan a potent stabilizing force.   How large are written the words "stabilization " and its antonyms " danger " and "pressure" on the pages of political history in the Far East since the Great War! The vigour of this young and growing Japan is concretely illustrated in her economic, cultural and military expansion.

3. REPLENISHMENT OF ECONOMIC POWER

The consumption power by a nation is fairly illustrated by the figures of its national budget. In the first year of Meiji (1868) the total budget of the Japanese Government was no more than 33,000,-000 yen.   In 1935 it was seventy times as large, namely 2,300,000,000 yen. The trade expansion of

Japan in the past four decades presents an astounding record. The total amount of imports and exports for 1935 was 5,700 million yen — fourteen times as large as compared with the figure for 1898, which was 382 million yen. The national income of Japan is estimated to have been 1,148 million yen in 1905, 10,600 million yen in 1930, the year before the Manchurian Incident. The figure continued to rise steadily so that in 1936 it amounted to 16,500 million yen.

The Manchurian Incident marked a new epoch for Japan in many ways. In comparison with 1913, the year before the Great War, 1933, the year after the Manchurian Incident, showed an increase of 382 per cent. in the productive power of Japanese industry, whereas the increase for America was 108 per cent. and for Great Britain, 87 per cent. The index numbers for the industrial consumption of electric power for 1935 against 100 for 1913 were 2,450 for Japan, 400 for America, and 464 for Great Britain, indicating the swift tempo of Japan's industrial development.

Further expansion was achieved in the period between the Manchurian Incident and the China Affair. The industrial output of Japan, which in

1930 totaled in value 5,954 million yen exceeded 10,800 million yen in 1935.   In the case of the textile industry, the figure leaped from 2,000 million to 3,300 million in the above-mentioned five years; in the metal industry, from 510 million to 1,880 million; and in the chemical industry, from 900 million to 1,810 million

The quantitative expansion of Japanese industry was accompanied naturally by certain qualitative changes.   For instance, a shift "from cotton to iron," which was noted for some time, has been rendered imperative by the conditions prevailing since the Manchurian Incident.   Accordingly, from 1932 onward nearly 20 per cent. of the total industrial capital has been applied to industrial planning.   As regards the estimated consumption of coal, whereas it was 25,960,000 tons for 1931, it was nearly double for 1936, the exact figure being 42,240,000 tons, of which the heavy industries consumed 7,000,000 tons; the chemical industry, 5,-300,000 tons; the railways, 3,970,000 tons and the textile industry, 3,690,000 tons.

The industrial expansion of Japan must be viewed in the light of the capital strength of the country.   To compare the total capital investments

among the leading nations in 1936, the figure for
America is 1,194 million dollars, for Great Britain
147 million pounds, for Germany 442 million
marks, for France 3,596 million francs and for
Japan 1,231 million yen. By computing these
sums at the current rate of exchange, even America,
the wealthiest nation on earth, had only four times
as large and Great Britain about twice as large an
industrial capital as Japan, while Germany and
France each had something like one half the
amount of Japan. The index number for the
world's industrial output against 100 for 1928, the
year prior to the universal panic, is 117.6 for 1936
and 126.9 for the first half of 1937. The following table gives the same index numbers for individual nations.

	1936	1937 (First half)
Japan	170.7	190.1
Great Britain	123.7	131.4
Germany	107.8	114.4
Italy	95.5	107.5
U.S.A.	94.6	105.0
France	77.8	81.5

These statistical figures require no further
comment in order to illustrate the industrial power

possessed by Japan, which constitutes the foundation of her national strength.

4. PROGRESS IN EDUCATION

Japan's ability to compete successfully with
Occidental nations in economic fields is not only
due to her abundant supply of man-power but also
to her well-organized educational system. According to a survey conducted in 1935, there were altogether 46,138 educational establishments from
elementary schools up to universities, attended by
more than 14,035,000 pupils and students. This
means that there are eleven schools to every 100
square-kilometres, or 20 students to every 100 per-
sons of the country's population. Particularly notable is the diffusion of elementary education, which
is compulsory and which is achieving quite fully
its purpose with 99.58 per cent. of the children of
school age at school.

It was in 1872 that the modern educational
system was instituted after the French pattern.
The country was divided into districts, each with its
university, middle schools, or elementary schools,
while normal schools, technical schools and foreign language schools were set up at various places.

The Imperial message issued at that time said,
"We expect that hereafter throughout Our land
there shall be no illiterate family in a village, and
no illiterate person in a household," and continued, "As regards higher learning it shall be left
to individual choice according to one's talent, but
it shall be unlawful not to send one's children,
without distinction of sex, to the elementary
school."

Since then the system has been reformed and
improved to suit the requirements of the changing
conditions of the country.   But in the rush of importing Western learning there were introduced
all sorts of doctrines and -isms without discrimina-
tion.   In order to eliminate this evil, the Imperial
Rescript on Education was issued in 1890, a unique
and monumental document, setting forth definitely
and permanently the principles of national education for Japan.

Aside from special popular institutions for the
training of youths who do not proceed regularly
from the elementary school to the middle school,
there were in 1935 the following public schools
and colleges under the control of the Ministry of
Education :

	number	attendance
Elementary schools	25,771	11,232,076
Middle schools	555	330,992
Girls' high schools	970	388,935
Vocational schools	1,069	342,914
Vocational continuation schools	15,306	1,281,814
High schools	32	18,905
Universities	45	71,162
Technical schools	117	70,083
Technical colleges	56	24,112
Normal schools	102	30,420
Normal colleges	2	1,775
Women's Normal colleges	2	815
Others	2,111	241,820
Total	46,138	14,035,823

There are, of course, many public libraries and museums. The total number of public and private libraries in 1935 was 4,794 with a total annual attendance of 24,660,000. There are also public lecture courses and educational facilities for adults and employees and workers. In fact, everything is being done for the full intellectual development of the nation.

5. PERFECTION OF NATIONAL DEFENCE

Modern warfare requires the mobilization of all the human and material resources of a nation.

The national economy must necessarily be reorganized and put on a wartime basis, especially the vital industrial power, which may well be regarded as the criterion of a nation's capacity for national defence. That is to say, under modern conditions, war is a highly capitalized industry requiring vast and manifold technical facilities.

The uncertain prospects of peace have brought on an armament race among the Powers. The United States, acting upon her policy of "armed neutrality," doubled her national defence appropriation in 1937 to 856 million dollars from 480 million in 1934. Great Britain inaugurated in February, 1936, a five-year plan of rearmament entailing an expenditure of 1,500 million pounds. Her armament budget grew from 158 million pounds for 1931-37 to 198 million pounds for 1937-38. As for Germany under Hitler, an enormous armament scheme was carried out, costing 15,800 million marks, between 1932 and the end of March, 1936, while her military appropriations for 1936-37 amounted to 7,000 million marks. Japan's military budget has also shown a marked increase since the Manchurian Incident.

The League of Nations as a peace organization, though regarded at first as a superb creation of man's wisdom, has proved itself but a frail structure built upon the shifting sands of realities. War, denounced and outlawed, does not cease any more than does the progress of mankind. War between organized communities or nations—especially civilized nations—originates always in political circumstances and is resorted to from political motives. Thus "war is not only a political action, but a political means and one form of the continuation of political relations between nations."

In the world of today, peace and justice, the highest political ideals, are not identical but exist as two intersecting circles, so to speak. There can be, therefore, peace without justice, and justice without peace. Before we attain the ideal of eternal peace, war will probably continue to be an unavoidable mode of political action.

In old Japan spears were always hung upon the wall of a samurai's house for instant use in time of war. But in ordinary times they served as a symbol of vigilance on the part of the occupants of the dwelling. This tension of being constantly on guard enlivened the atmosphere of the household with no small degree of vigour and health.

The armament of a nation is a symbol of the nation's tense energy, which may be released in peace time for the ceaseless creation of cultural values. It also embodies the Japanese philosophy of "the sword that slays not" by forestalling any occasion for resorting to armed force.

The Japanese official text book on warfare begins with the sentence, "The first aim of battle is to overwhelm and annihilate the enemy," and goes on to say, "victory depends upon the employment of fighting power, or upon a superior combination of spiritual power and material power." It is this principle that has been put into practice by the land, sea and air forces of Japan in the present campaign in China.

Spiritual power is described as consisting of "mutual confidence between commanders and the rank and file, the strict maintenance of discipline, and the manifestation of the soldier spirit in faithful service to the Throne and to the country." And this is no other than Bushido—the way of the warrior—with its precious tradition of centuries.

Material power lies in "skill of scientific application of technical ability and material means of war." This material power has been amply demonstrated by our fleets that dominate the China coast from Tientsin to Canton, by our air forces which have frequently been compelled to fight against great odds hundreds of miles from their landing fields, and by our mechanized units which have enabled our Army to overcome the severe handicaps resulting from the numerical superiority of the enemy and the vastness of the war areas.

The growth of Japan's material fighting power may be traced by examining the expenditure for national defence in the past. The military appropriation for 1893, the year just before the Sino-Japanese War, was 14,700,000 yen. In forty-three years, namely in 1936, the figure rose to 727,000,-000 yen. In the same period the naval appropriation rose from 8,100,000 yen to 683,000,000 yen, which means an increase by eighty times. It is the national strength of an ever-expanding Japan that has rendered possible such expenditures.

6. JAPAN'S AXES OF ECONOMIC EXPANSION AND NATIONAL DEFENCE

Japan has expanded, and she is expanding still. The numerical increase and the cultural advance of our people are the results of the growth of the

inner life of the race.   In the course of their economic and cultural progress the Japanese have
made their country an organic whole and have
systematized their national economy on a rational
basis by virtue of the continuity of the economic
body, the unity of the economic structure, the im-
mutability of the economic area, and the adaptability of the character of economic life.

The Japanese archipelago, stretching over 4,-
800 kilometres from Shimushu Island in the north
to Kasho Island south of Taiwan, forms a line run-
ning from the arctic zone to the tropic.   It is the
base-line of Japanese economic development.

The ports of Osaka and Kobe, which attract
ships to the extent of 52,557,000 tons a year, surpassing by far Yokohama, the gateway to Tokyo,
with its annual trade of only 16,346,000 tons, constitute obviously the greatest centre of commerce
and industry in Japan.   And Osaka is located almost in the middle of the above-mentioned Japanese economic base-line.

Since the former German colonies in the
South Seas were placed under Japanese mandate,
Japan's rule has been extended over the Northern
Pacific Ocean to the equator itself.   From Jaluit

Island, situated in the extreme southwest of the mandated territory, the shortest route to the above-mentioned Japanese economic base-line — a line drawn at right angles thereto — will meet it at Osaka.

Again a similar line drawn from the town of Manchouli, which is on the northwestern border of Manchoukuo and is a junction point of the North Manchuria Railway with the Trans-Siberian Railway, occupying the most important strategic position, will also meet the Japanese economic base-line at Osaka. This means that a straight line linking Jaluit Island and the Manchurian town intersects at right angles with the Japanese economic base-line at Osaka, the commercial and industrial metropolis of Japan. Just as the importance of Manchoukuo to Japan is largely military, as is obvious from the Japan-Manchoukuo Protocol providing for the common defence of that country, and the presence of large Japanese forces therein, so the importance of the South Seas Islands from a naval point of view may be readily grasped by recalling the provisions in the Four-Power Treaty concluded between Japan, America, Great Britain and France in 1921 and the Washington

Treaty of 1922, restricting the fortification of islands in those waters.   The Jaluit-Manchouli line
is, therefore, Japan's base-line of national defence.

Curiously enough the two base-lines of Japan's
economic life and of her national defence form
rectangular axes of co-ordinates having for their
focus Osaka, the very centre of her commerce and
industry.   And it is these Japanese axes which illustrate graphically the economic and political situation of East Asia.   Japan has become the stabilizing force of East Asia through the formation of
these axes, a process which was completed with
the close of the Manchurian Incident.   It may be
regarded as providential that these rectangular axes
of co-ordinates have been brought into being to
symbolize the actual strength and position of Japan
as the leader of Asia.

CHAPTER II

THE EVOLUTION OF JAPANESE CIVILIZATION

1. THE SPIRITUAL DEVELOPMENT OF JAPAN

WE hear of the time when "earth and heaven were parted and grass and trees spoke human tongues," and of the generations of gods who gave birth to the islands and performed many other prodigious feats. Out of this shining mist of mythology the Japanese people emerge into history as a nation organized into many clans and governed by a supreme ruler—a "Manifest God." The Yamato race—the progenitor and nucleus of our nation —formed one large family of which the Sovereign was the Head. And it is this system that has persisted to this day and constitutes the foundation of the unique national polity of Japan.

Jimmu, the first Emperor, on ascending the Throne, declared his intention to "make the world one household," a cosmopolitan ideal which has always animated our nation. The sanctity of the Imperial House and the unswerving loyalty of the people have their origin in the remotest periods of our race. These traditions and beliefs and the racial qualities — courage, self-sacrifice, and the love of nature, purity and cleanliness, all derived from the "Divine Age"—are what characterize the Japanese people as a unique nation in the Orient and in the world.

Japan has, however, grown in stature and strength by assiduously absorbing and assimilating the civilization of China and in more recent times that of the Occident. The importation of continental culture was greatly accelerated through the conquest of Korea in the 3rd century after Christ. By the beginning of the 8th century the court at Nara was in direct contact with the Chinese courts of the Sui and Tang dynasties, to which official embassies were despatched from time to time.

The great Reform of Taika in the year 645 was modelled largely on the governmental system and institutions of China under the Tang dynasty, which then was at the height of its power and glory, holding sway over a vast territory extending from Korea to Turkestan, and from Mongolia to Annam. The brilliant arts and letters of the continent were bodily transported into Japan. In the Imperial City of Nara, laid out according to the grandiose scale of the Chinese capital of Changan, there rose magnificent palaces and temples. In a sense Nara's brilliance was a reflection of the still greater light on the continent. It was the early Tang Empire that helped the Japanese to gain the concept of a world State and to acquire the capacity for tolerance and the ability to embrace and control alien peoples. And it was in this period that Buddhism, first introduced into Japan in the 6th century in the reign of the Emperor Kimmei, began to spread over the country, partly through the patriotic appeal of certain passages in the Books of Golden Light, and of the Benevolent King and other sutras which were believed to be desirable for safe-guarding the country against evil fortune.

In the succeeding Heian Period (7th-13th centuries), reaction set in against the domination of Chinese influence, and there was a conscious, and to a great extent a successful, attempt to create a more purely Japanese art and literature. The famous Tales of the Genji and other writings of those brilliant court ladies are products of this period.

In the field of religion, Kobo Daishi introduced the Shingon Sect which taught that the Dai-
nichi Nyorai was the proto-Buddha of whom all
other Buddhas and Bodhisattvas were partial mani-
festations. This doctrine completely reconciled
Buddhism with the native cult of Shinto, according to which all things in the universe are derived
from the central deity — *Ame no Minakanushi no
Mikoto*—who had been brought into being through
the creative power, called Musubi. The "eight
hundred thousand" gods who people the heaven
and earth are secondary and multiple manifesta-
tions of the one divine being who pervades the
universe. The Tendai—another sect brought from
China by Saicho—preached the presence of Bud-
dhahood in all things and the pervasion of nature
by one common life—a doctrine which confirmed
the ancient Japanese belief in the communion held
between man and nature.

Buddhism was finally and fully naturalized on
Japanese soil with the founding of such popular
sects as the Nichiren-shu, the Jodo-shu, and the
Shin-shu, respectively by Nichiren, Honen and
Shinran, in the Kamakura Period. These sects
still command a far greater following than the

more occult and learned branches of Buddhism that were imported from China in earlier periods.

Side by side with Buddhism, Confucianism made its way into Japan. This venerable code of conduct, taught by the Chinese sage 3,000 years ago and expounded by the philosophers and scholars of later ages, has left indelible marks on the character of the Japanese race. Confucian studies throve most in the feudal periods, especially during the Tokugawa Shogunate, under the patronage of both Shoguns and daimyos. There stands at Yushima in Tokyo to-day the Seido, a shrine dedicated to Confucius.

Such has been the progress of our spiritual life, which has been constantly and consciously nourished and enriched from alien sources. How the new Japan since the Meiji Restoration has adopted the civilization of the West and yet preserved and enhanced her ancient national spirit and ideal, is a matter well-known to all the world. This infinite capacity for tolerance and assimilation on the part of the Japanese nation serves only to explain its infinite capacity for expansion, which in turn reveals the national ideal "to make the world one household."

2. PROGRESS OF SCIENCE

The Asiatic pattern of their minds has caused the imagination of the Japanese to turn more to the things of the spirit than to the physical and objective world. The generalization does not, however, imply a lack of scientific spirit or talent in the Japanese. The architectural wonders of Nara—of which the Horyuji temple with its five-storied pagoda is one of the surviving specimens —would have been impossible without considerable scientific knowledge — especially in kinetics and mathematics.

In view of the fact that mathematical intuition and aptitude constitute the basic requirement of scientific progress, it is interesting to recall that as early as the beginning of the 8th century the Japanese court had its " Professor of Mathematics " to train students. The use of the abacus was popularized in the 16th century. It is recorded the Shogun Tokugawa Yoshimune devised an astronomical instrument in order to study the movements of celestial bodies. Especially notable is the fact that one, Seki Kowa, a mathematician, who was a contemporary of Newton and Leibnitz, invented calculus in his Japanese way of reckoning.

But the real progress of science in Japan commenced with the Restoration of Meiji, when modern schools and universities and technical colleges were established and students were sent abroad. A marvellous degree of progress has been achieved since then, so that Japan to-day can hold her own among the most advanced countries of Europe and America in all branches of science as is demonstrated by the impressive list of Japanese discoveries and inventions.

In mathematics, Dr. Dairoku Kikuchi and Dr. Rikitaro Fujisawa, who distinguished themselves by their brilliant scholastic records at the University of Cambridge, returned to Japan to teach higher mathematics and laid the foundation for the place Japan occupies to-day in this branch of science. The numerous dissertations by Dr. Tsuruichi Hayashi on modern mathematics, the treatise by Dr. Teiichi Takagi on complex multiplication, the treatise by Dr. Eitaro Sakai on the multiplication theories of elliptical functions and the researches conducted by Dr. Soichi Kakeya on the subject of simultaneous integral equations and the theory of functions are a few of the monumental achievements accomplished by Japanese mathematicians.

In physics Drs. Aikitsu Tanakadate, Hanyu-chi Muraoka and Hantaro Nagaoka, disciples of Professor Ewing, returned from Europe in 1882. Dr. Nagaoka discovered, while still a student, the fact that the pole of nickel varies in the process of magnetization and became a pioneer investigator in that field.   Dr. Kotaro Honda is one of the world's foremost authorities on magnetic steel. There are also noted specialists such as Dr. Jun Ishihara on theoretical studies, Dr. K. Tawara on Japanese swords and Dr. Yuzuru Hiraga on high-speed vessels.

Dr. Shinzo Shinjo, a great authority on astro-nomical physics, has published the results of his profound researches on the nature of the universe, while the discovery by Dr. Sakae Mizusawa of the Mizusawa Observatory regarding the variations of the earth's axis has attracted wide attention.   Drs. Fusakichi Omori and Akitsune Imamura as seis-mologists are well-known throughout the world.

In the first year of Meiji (1868) the first chem-ical laboratory was established in Osaka, where analyses and simple experiments relating to the chemical industry were conducted under the guidance of a foreigner. It was from such modest beginnings that chemical science in Japan has developed into what it is to-day, producing such noted scholars as Dr. Joji Sakurai and Dr. Tomomasa Heiwa. The latter completed in rapid succession useful research experiments concerning the compounds of nitrogen and sulphur, contributing thereby to the amazing development of the nitrogen industry in Japan. The perfection of the method of producing artificial silk by Messrs. S. Hoshino and S. Yamamoto and the success of Dr. K. Takahashi in the isolation of vitamin A are also achievements worthy of note.

Numerous are the inventions and discoveries by Japanese which have directly benefitted various branches of industry and engineering, among which may be mentioned the Miyahara waterpipe boiler, considered the best of its kind in the world ; the device for stabilizing vessels invented by Dr. Shintaro Motora ; the Toyoda automatic loom, which is responsible for the world-wide advance of Japanese cotton goods ; Mikimoto cultured pearls ; and the K. S. steel and M. S. steel produced by Dr. Honda.

Finally, Japan has made notable contributions to medical science. The Kitazato Institute for the study of infectious diseases is unsurpassed in equipment and personnel, while the discovery of dysentery bacilli by Dr. Kiyoshi Shiga marks an epoch in the history of bacteriology. The mere mention of the very names of Dr. Jokichi Takamine and Dr. Hideo Noguchi is sufficient to indicate the calibre of the scientific genius working for the creation of the new Japan.

3. JAPAN OLD, BUT EVER NEW

The past seventy years, during which Japan made the startling progress described above, were marked with constant conflict and confusion in the field of thought. But bitter as was the conflict and trying as was the confusion, the results have been beneficial. Chastened and refined in this crucible of affliction, there has risen the soul of Japan, stronger and nobler than ever.

The first few years of the Meiji Era saw the reactionary forces of an ill-advised conservatism opposed to equally ill-advised but powerful forces in favour of Westernization. The rift grew wider as the conservatives formed a common front with the

German school of nationalism to confront those who advocated political reform in the direction of liberty and enfranchisement, and finally divided the nation into two camps, nationalism on the one hand and democracy on the other. In February, 1889, the Constitution was promulgated. As soon as people learned the intrinsic difference between this Constitution, granted by the Emperor, and those of England, France and other countries, great was the disappointment among the ardent followers of Montesquieu and Rousseau. The voices of the radicals were suddenly stilled, for there was no longer any room left for political agitation save for controversy on the interpretation of the Constitution. With the decline of the radical reformers, there came to prevail throughout the nation a certain type of thinking closely akin to the German type of political philosophy.

Nevertheless, the Imperial Constitution failed to quell the storm in the social and educational fields. The forces of Westernization, including Christianity, continued to carry on a furious three-cornered battle with the schools of national classicism and of Confucianism until there was issued in 1891 the Imperial Rescript on Education.

While the Constitution provided a careful and well-elaborated modern system of government of an Occidental type, the Imperial Rescript on Education was intended to elucidate the eternal virtues of old Japan. Exhorting the nation to loyalty, patriotism and solidarity, the Rescript put a healthy check upon the overzealous campaigners for "liberty and equality." Japan awoke from her infatuation with the Occident, and nationalism, fast sweeping over the country, clashed with the church. In 1892 Dr. Tetsujiro Inouye attacked the anti-national character of Christianity, giving rise to a heated controversy between educators and missionaries. Though the war ended without a decisive battle, the church was led, as a result, to assume a more Japanese complexion in both spirit and organization.

Side by side with the ascendancy of nationalism there arose the cult of individualism in the last decade of the 19th century. The works of Nietzche and of Schopenhauer were read. The problems of faith and the doctrine of naturalism perturbed the Japanese mind. Finally, socialism appeared on the scene. Socialism, as an outward manifestation of a newly-awakened individualism, cropped up in Japan early in the second decade of the Meiji Era. The movement gained headway as the result of the notable progress of the working class in the years following the Sino-Japanese War of 1894-95, during which the writings of Saint-Simon, Brieux, and Marx were read extensively, so that by the time of the Russo-Japanese War (1904-05) Japanese Socialists actually launched an anti-war campaign. The extraordinary growth of capitalism after the Russian War stimulated all the more the propagation of socialist thoughts, culminating in the anarchist-socialist plot of 1910. Despite the rigid surveillance exercised by the authorities, the establishment of Soviet Russia brought on an epoch of unprecedented activity on the part of Marxian Socialists, hoisting the banner of "class warfare." On the other hand, the nationalists were by no means willing to be overridden. Vigorous anti-socialist movements were started to counter every socialistic doctrine imported from abroad. It was amid such intense clashes and baffling confusion of thought that Japan found herself on the eve of the Manchurian Incident.

European culture is extraneous; and it lays emphasis upon organizations and systems. Its

honest positivism has led to scientific progress and
the flowering of modern material civilization.   It
is an undeniable fact that the Japanese were first
dazzled and misled by the glamour of this external
civilization, and that in the course of their contact
with it they came to have a realistic, utilitarian and
even mercenary outlook on life, giving rise to the
worship of Mammon which became alarmingly
rife after the war with Russia.   With the individualism of the earlier period replaced by naturalism, Japan was flooded for a time with the works
of Flaubert, Zola and Maupassant.   The tension
of the Manchurian Incident cleared the air of these
conflicting doctrines, revealing Japan's real soul
which had been submerged for years under chaotic
confusion and tumult in the world of thought.

Viewed from its results, Marxism has helped
the Japanese to weigh the virtues and shortcomings
of capitalism and has implanted in the younger
generation a keen and vivid sense of social justice.
The doctrines of Tolstoi, Kropotkin, Prud'hon
and Bakunin influenced the creative Japan only
as agencies for pointing to something nobler and
more beautiful than themselves.   After all, Nietzche, Zola, and Maupassant did not prove potent

enough to contaminate the virile blood of the Japanese, who were more influenced by the healthy and beneficent ideas of Dante, Goethe and Shakespeare.

Old Japan was a disciple of Confucius and Buddha while she also consulted Mencius, Hsuntse, Chuhsi and Wang Yang-ming. New Japan was taught by Plato and Aristotle; she studied Kant, Fichte, Hegel and Spinoza, turning then to Rousseau and Montesquieu. With a courage born of conviction she proceeded to remodel and reorganize her national life along the lines of her national ideal. Such untoward incidents as those of May 15, 1932, and February 26, 1936, were not altogether unexpected in a young Japan fired with a great zeal for justice and impatient with the slow changes of time. Deplorable as these events were, they did help to make the leaders of Japan realize that there were certain fundamental maladjustments in the nation's life which had to be corrected.

While Europe with its positivism and scientific spirit grew rich and powerful and dominated the world, imposing its own world outlook upon others, Asia has all the while been striving to build a spiritual empire upon its deathless ideal.   What is needed for humanity is the simultaneous fulfilment or fusion of both these European and Asiatic aims.

The new scientific civilization and the old ideal of " the world, one household " that lives in the hearts of the people—these constitute the outstanding features of present-day Japan.   Japan, new, yet ever old, must be the hope of Asia and of the world.

CHAPTER III

JAPAN AND THE ASIATIC CONTINENT

1. THE PRESENT STAGE OF JAPAN'S CONTINENTAL EXPANSION

THE history of Japan's economic, cultural and military progress reveals the interesting principle and process of racial expansion. Our people, grown large in numbers and highly developed in civilization, were bound to break through their territorial confines and penetrate into the world outside. This penetration was not accomplished always with ease but was often attended by considerable friction and conflict. It is there that we find the life-force of a race. It is there that we hear of the "danger spots of world population" and "population pressure in the Far East."

"Japan gets cotton from India and China, iron ore from China, the Malay Peninsula and the Philippines, and agricultural and mining products from Manchoukuo. Even to-day Australia and New Zealand are exporting wool to Japan while

there are good prospects for sending iron ore from
Western Australia.   On the other hand, Japan's
shipping and the cheap cotton goods and other
articles made in Japan are widely used.   The development of trade is far more real than the vague
notions of Pan-Asianism in politics.'' So says an
author on population.   The penetrative power of
the Japanese race must first of all be studied from
the angle of trade.

The index of the total volume for Japan's foreign trade, taking that of 1913 as 100, showed a
steady increase with but slight occasional variations
until it amounted to 244.4 (unit price index, 157)
in import and to 309.5 in export (unit price index,
111.2) in 1938.   The following table gives the total
values of Japan's exports to and imports from North
America, Europe and Asiatic countries for the
years 1913 and 1933 :

Region	Exports		Imports	
	1913	1933	1913	1933
North America	190	499	97	669
Europe	147	182	158	283
China	218	435	92	284
India	30	146	173	205
Rest of Asia	—	98	40	139

* Unit, one million yen.

The increase of Japan's trade with Asiatic countries became more marked from 1932 onward, after the Manchurian Incident, as may be seen in the table below :

Region	Exports (unit, one million yen)					Imports (unit, one million yen)				
	1931	1932	1933	1934	1935	1931	1932	1933	1934	1935
Asia	505	677	930	1,169	1,304	493	450	658	812	869
Europe	104	127	182	227	262	199	225	282	295	352
N. America	442	459	515	450	579	378	550	668	824	870
S. America	10	13	30	61	73	7	4	12	23	42
Africa	58	85	137	182	183	18	27	48	79	69
Oceania	26	47	65	79	95	117	139	211	214	248

Trade expansion went hand in hand with the expansion of the shipping industry.   In 1903 before the Russo-Japanese War, Japan had only 650,-000 tons of vessels, which grew to 1,030,400 by the end of 1906.   The Great War raised Japan's shipping industry to third place in the world, the tonnage rising from 1,593,000 in 1913 to 3,050,000 in 1920.   And by 1934 the figures grew further to 3,860,000 tons.   Before the Great War the ordinary speed of Japanese vessels was 9 knots, whereas in recent years they have attained a speed of 18 knots, a fact which accelerates greatly the process of Japanese penetration on the continent.

Moreover, in China Japan maintains a shipping service on the Yangtze River ; and in Manchoukuo she operates for the Manchoukuo Government 8,800 kilometres of railway, besides her own 1,100 kilometres represented by the South Manchuria Railway.

Japan's trade expansion occasioned a " cotton war " with Lancashire in the Indian market, a boycott in the Dutch East Indies, and the imposition of a prohibitive tariff by Australia on Japanese goods.   However, these difficulties have been, or are in process of being, successfully overcome by diplomatic means.

As regards the advance of Japanese capital on the Asiatic continent, some 2,800 million yen have been poured into Manchuria as a direct capital investment, while 1,000 million yen are invested in China in cultural enterprises as well as in loans and direct investments, as compared with 56 million yen in the northern Pacific, 92 million yen in the South Seas, and 120 million yen in South America. Finally, it should be noted that in the past five years Japanese emigrants numbered some 300,000, of whom the Asiatic Continent has absorbed more than two-thirds.

Japanese penetration by means of emigration and capital investment is directed in the main towards the Asiatic Continent; and it is injecting fresh vitality and power into the community of Asiatic races.

Japan's expansion into the Asiatic mainland has been motivated not only by the necessity to improve conditions at home, but also as a defensive measure to forestall the danger of aggression from the continent, for the proximity of the Korean peninsula leaves Japan forever exposed to attacks from this direction.

It is a matter of history that any race which wins supremacy over China will conquer Korea, and will then try to invade Japan across the straits. In the earliest period of her history Japan felt the pressure of the Suchens in the north across the Japan Sea, and she has constantly faced the threat of a continental Power lurking behind Korea. Most of the civil disorders experienced by Japan prior to the complete unification of the Island Empire were occasioned by rebellious elements in league with one power or another on the continent.

The campaign of Abe Hirafu in Northern Japan in 658 A.D. in the reign of the Empress

Saimei and the subsequent expedition he led against
the Suchen invasion from the Continent; the
expeditions against the Ezo in Eastern Japan by
Prince Yamato-takeru and Sakanoe Tamuramaro;
the conquest of the Kumaso tribe in Kyushu by
Prince Yamato-takeru, and the Korean expedition
of the Empress Jingu were all undertaken with a
view to removing the continental menace abroad
or to eradicating this very source of civil distur-
bance.

In 1019 the Nuchens with a fleet of fifty ships
invaded the islands of Iki and Tsushima and attempted to land on the northern coast of Kyushu.
The famous Mongol Invasion was still another attempt on the part of a continental Power to conquer Japan. Kublai Khan, after having built his
mammoth world empire straddling over Asia and
Europe, wanted to add the Japanese archipelago
to the list of his conquests. However, his large
expeditionary forces despatched in 1274 and again
in 1281 failed, owing to the valiant defence put up
by Japanese frontier forces and to the "Divine
Wind," or typhoon, that completely wrecked the
Mongol armada.

Conspicuous in the subsequent history of

Japan's relations with the continent have been the Korean expedition of Toyotomi Hideyoshi in the sixteenth century, the advocacy of Korean invasion by Saigo and his followers in the early years of Meiji, the wars with China and Russia, and more recently the Manchurian Incident of 1931 and finally the present China Affair.

These events in every instance signified Japan's efforts to repel in self-defence the pressure from the continent. At the same time they have resulted in the actual advance of the Japanese race onto the continent. The Korean peninsula and Manchuria, which had so long provided a convenient passage for the continental armies marching on Japan, have now been turned into corridors for Japanese expansion in China.

Japan's influence, as represented graphically in her co-ordinate axes of economic expansion and national defence, extends over a vast territory in East Asia. In Manchuria where once at the risk of her very existence Japan fought against the southward advance of Russian imperialism, she now commands an impregnable position both militarily and economically by virtue of the special and inseparable relations which she maintains with

Manchoukuo. From this base Japan's penetration
into North China has been but an inevitable step
in the course of her racial expansion.

2. ALIEN INVASIONS OF CHINA OVER THE GREAT WALL

In the "Book of the Latter Han" it is written : "Heaven made mountains and rivers, the
Tsin built the Great Wall and the Han erected
forts and barriers—all this for the purpose of sepa-
rating the interior from the exterior and keeping
apart different customs and manners." The Great
Wall of China, constructed more than two thousand years ago by the first emperor of the Tsin
dynasty, is really an embodiment of Chinese anti-
foreignism. But the dynamics of racial expansion
scarcely knows border and barrier, be they natural
or artificial. The Great Wall of the Tsin Emperor
has proved to be only a colossal monument to com-
memorate the repeated incursions of northern
tribes into China. The so-called "barbarians"
inhabiting the Mongolian steppes and the Manchurian plains were the ones who imposed alien
rule upon the Han race from time to time by
founding such dynasties of their own as the Liao,

the Chin, the Yuan of the Mongols under Kublai Khan, and the Tsin of the Manchus which was in power until 1912.   That these northern races, attracted by richer soil and better climate, and tempted by the glamour of a higher civilization, should invade China whenever they had the chance was inevitable.   It is the universal law of migration throughout the history of mankind.

At the same time, the Han race, with its superior civilization and its immense capacity for assimilation, though bowing often to the barbarian sword, succeeded always in preserving its own culture, its social order and its racial integrity.   In fact, the Hans, by absorbing and assimilating the invaders, emerged in the end the virtual victors infused with new blood and fresh vitality.   Thus has the history of China shown frequent repetition of the same drama with the Hans and the northern invaders fighting for political and military supremacy, while the stage-setting of Chinese civilization remained unchanged.

After the Sino-Japanese and the Russo-Japanese Wars the situation was rapidly modified. Manchuria, a "barbarian desert" of old days, over which had roamed nomadic tribes, was transformed into a land of 30,000,000 people, producing each year 867 million bushels of corn and possessing a fine network of railways, the like of which was to be found nowhere in China proper. Now, with Manchoukuo as an ally of Japan, there has come into being something like a military and economic bloc in East Asia, and the new nation is being fast industrialized with a view to the production of vital materials.

The energy stored in this new reservoir is bound to overflow and stream southward. That nothing can check the flood is proved by history. The Hans are again making a futile attempt to stop by force the inevitable advance of a race taking its rise beyond the Great Wall.

CHAPTER IV

SIGNIFICANCE OF THE CHINA AFFAIR
IN HISTORY

1. THE RÔLE OF JAPAN IN CHINA

THE earth was once inhabited by huge uncouth reptiles. They prospered well, as may be gathered from the size and the numbers of their fossils that are being discovered in a certain geological stratum. But they became extinct, unable to live in the new environment of a new age.

The Chinese people once spread over the fertile valleys of the Yellow River and the Yangtzekiang, replacing the Miao tribe in central China. They built up the world empires of the Hans and the Tangs and created a glorious civilization of their own. But after having outlived their age and the environment, they have been conquered repeatedly by alien races from beyond the Great Wall. They have deteriorated in racial quality and stamina. Their "Middle Flowery Kingdom" of old is now but a dreary land devoid of trees

where the great rivers cause untold loss of life and
property every year through flood and famine.
China in recent decades has been reduced to a
quasi-colonial state, barely escaping extinction under the pressure and exploitation of imperialistic
Powers.

Japan, on the contrary, is a growing nation,
full of life and energy. She has in the course of
her development absorbed all that was good in Chinese culture and civilization. She has also adopted
and assimilated Occidental science and arts, as has
already been described, while preserving intact her
ancient spiritual heritage. It is this very old and
yet very new race which is confronting China to-
day in order to bring about a historic change in
her national career. This should not be taken in
the same sense as the descent of a barbarian tribe
across the Great Wall.

China has been able in the past to absorb and
tame the northern races which conquered her land.
The Japanese, however, are a more civilized nation
and a more virile race, and this power of penetration is not to be compared with that of a barbarian
horde boasting only of superiority in horseman-
ship or of skill in shooting arrows. Herein lies

the unique character of the present advance of the
Japanese into China.   The old Great Wall is of
no use.   In the twentieth century the Japanese
nation, as a bulwark against Communism, constitutes a real Great Wall for China.

2. EXPANSION FOR SELF-DEFENCE AND CULTURE

Japan expands onto the continent.   Call it
"imperialism," if you like, but the historic significance of Japanese imperialism must not be forgotten.

Japan has fought several wars in self-defence
against aggression from the mainland, but signifi-
cantly enough Japan has at the same time converted
this road of military aggression from the continent
into a highway for her own pacific penetration of
that region.

The Oriental ideal of love, benevolence and
mutual help condemns war for selfish ends.   Japan's
armament—always a "divine sword that slays not"
—is dedicated to the peace of East Asia and to the
welfare of the world ; it is employed only against
the forces inimical to international justice and to
the common interests of East Asia.   Japan's advance, inspired by humanity, should not be con-

fused with aggression for gain at the expense of other nations.

The external factors of Japanese expansion are three — namely, the increase of population, the growth of economic power and the necessity of securing peace as a pre-requisite for this economic progress. "Whosoever hath, to him shall be given, and he shall have more abundance; but whosoever hath not, from him shall be taken away even that which he hath." If these words are to be taken as a definition of the present day world under imperialism or monopolistic capitalism — Japan is rather on the side of him who has not and who is in fear of losing what he has. That any one should own property is to be accepted as a reasonable principle, but the possession of super-abundance beyond one's capacity for administration, is not only a social crime but a burden on one's self. An ugly aspect of present day imperialism, as revealed in the discussions on the redistribution of colonies, is the futile attempt on the part of the "grown" nations to check the "growing" nations. As the late Colonel House said, Japan has the right to demand an outlet for her population, and there is no reason why Japan should not be permitted to exploit some of the undeveloped territories still left on the globe, make them productive and increase thereby the wealth and happiness of mankind.

Obviously in these days when the world's economy has been placed under the " bloc " system with its high customs tariffs and other trade barriers, Japan is entitled to find some outlet for her surplus energy so as to assure her national existence. Japan's continental expansion, therefore, should be considered not so much as a capitalistic necessity but as a mission for the general cause of Asiatic civilization. Japan is not seeking to conquer the continent ; what she desires is common economic progress and political security based upon the co-operation and collaboration of the Asiatic peoples. Take, for instance, Manchoukuo. There flies the flag of the new state—an emblem of concord and harmony among its five races. Japan fosters no racial prejudices there. Neither does she oppress or exploit any group. There exists a relationship of perfect amity and of complete equality and reciprocity between Manchoukuo and Japan.

Japan's creative expansion on the continent

will be accompanied by the natural growth of a mutually beneficial economic unification. Unfortunately, however, ideals are never attained without incessant conflict with reality.

Behind the back of China and Japan with their ideals of universal concord and brotherhood, of benevolence and mutual help, of self-discipline and social order, there stalks Russian Communism. The Communist doctrine is built upon a materialistic interpretation of history; it repudiates religion, the sanctity of the home, and all the traditions and institutions that are the most precious heritages of mankind; it aims at a world revolution and the establishment of proletarian supremacy through class warfare.

The Communist International with its headquarters at Moscow is directing its nefarious operations with a view to undermining the peace and order of the world. Japan is compelled to take proper measures to combat the menace of the Comintern's operations in the Far East. Here is another important reason for Japan's advance on the Asiatic continent in the defence of civilization.

The recent Tokyo-Berlin-Rome Pact has set a new goal for mankind. Japan as the champion of East Asia, leading the crusade against Communism, has a mission of vital significance in history. Only by beating back the Red tide surging from beyond China's Great Wall will it be possible to insure the peace of East Asia and to enable its peoples to continue on the road of modern civilization. Metaphorically speaking, Japan has been compelled to assume the rôle of the Great Wall in order to check the barbarian invasion of the Reds.

Japan's imperialism is, therefore, in no way monopolistic. The objective of Japanese expansion is neither the attainment of capitalistic supremacy nor the acquisition of colonies, but the realization of harmony and concord among the nations of East Asia and the promotion of their common happiness and prosperity.

CHAPTER V

THE PRINCIPLES OF SINO-JAPANESE CO-OPERATION

1. JAPANESE PHILOSOPHY OF MUSUBI

VIEWED in the light of its historical precedents and character and also in the light of its cultural mission, expansion on the continent is the destiny of our race. China attempted to block Japan's path by resorting to force. This fatal miscalculation on the part of the Kuomintang Government, which relied too confidently on their own fighting strength and under-estimated the real power of Japan, has brought on the present disastrous conflict.

A Chinese philosopher of the 16th century in his book called "Tsaikontan", which is still widely read in China and Japan, has the following to say: "Wake up and discover your mistake! By discovering your mistake, turn away from it. You may thus convert misfortune into a blessing. You may then find life in death." China should realize her mistake ; she should appreciate fully the significance of the Japanese advance, examining calmly and carefully its underlying spirit; and she should, by awakening to the common obligations of all Asiatic peoples, try to make a fresh start.

The Japanese people desire only to live an active and abundant life in a world of peace and justice. They are considered to be a race highly complex in their racial composition, carrying in their blood certain elements of the Malay and the Polynesian, as well as of the ancient races of the Asiatic continent and the indigenous stock of the Ainu. In the course of their evolution as a distinct race, the Japanese under the influence of their natural environment and their varying and exhilarating climate acquired a love of beauty and purity. They lived close to nature, jealously protecting themselves against uncleanliness, both in body and in mind.

As children of the gods, our ancients lived in harmony with nature, acquiring a free and liberal social outlook which has developed into the ideal of universal brotherhood ("the world, one household"). At the same time, perceiving in the forces of nature the operation of a mysterious power, they formulated the philosophy of "Musubi." This philosophical concept is not a product of any single mind, and it has no formula or system. It is a belief which evolved from the experience of the race. By observing the unbroken rotation of the seasons and the happy multiplication of living creatures, our ancestors perceived the existence of a power or principle which operates in nature, creating, nourishing and multiplying all manner of things. They called this power *Musubi*. The word which is cognate with the verb *Musubu* (to unite, or join) is sometimes regarded as a compound of the two words, *musu* (to ferment) and *hi* (fire or heat), that is, a life-giving energy. Musubi thus signifies the function of a creative love that fosters life. It is the cosmic principle which brings abundance to life and magnifies truth and beauty. The ancient salute, *Iyasaka* (Prosper ever !), is expressive of the spirit of the Musubi.

The history of the Japanese nation is nothing but a record of the development of their faith in nature—the harmonization and self-identification of the race with its national environment.

Let us recall the cultural illumination of the Asuka and the Nara Periods with their glorious

cosmic oneness

art and architecture.   The solemn temples and
towers, the palaces and mansions, which arose on
the Yamato Plains surrounded by green-wooded
hills and mountains, were arranged in perfect
harmony with the natural surroundings so that
there was not a single pine or cherry tree that
seemed out of place.   In fact, it was scarcely possible to tell just where nature ended and art began,
so complete was the fusion of the two.   This characteristic is even more notable in the architecture
of the Heian Period and the succeeding eras.   To
quote from "The History of Japanese Culture"
by Dr. Nishida: "The beauty of the architecture
of the middle and later Heian Period was con-
siderably enhanced through the unity of the buildings and their environment.   The Hoshoji Temple
of Shirakawa was erected amid limpid streams and
placid lakes in the shadow of steep hills, and possessed gardens of its own planted with tall trees.
The Byodoin built by Prime Minister Yorimichi
commanded a magnificent view of the Uji River
shooting through a precipitous gorge, while the
Konjiki-in, a temple built by the Empress Consort
of the Emperor Shijo, was sequestered deep in a
mountain hollow.   That these ornate and brilliant

buildings set in the heart of nature did not destroy
the scenic beauty was due to the spirit of the Fuji-
wara Period." This spirit lives still; it is the Japanese attitude of mind toward nature.

Preserve nature and re-discover oneself in
nature ! — so teaches the philosophy of Musubi.
It is not destruction; it is creation and synthesis.
By obliterating the line between individual selves,
Musubi recreates a greater self.

From the beginning of their history the Japanese people, as children of nature, pure and in-
nocent, simple and unsophisticated, have constantly
practised the doctrine of Musubi. They have
grown by negation of self and through fusion and
synthesis. The China Affair will after all prove
an occasion for the birth of a new life through the
operation of Musubi.

2. MUSUBI AND THE CHINA AFFAIR

A Marxist may dismiss the subject of Japan's
continental expansion simply as a manifestation of
monopolistic capitalism in its final stage. The so-
called scientific analysis of history is apt to ascribe
to a simple event a complexity of character which
it does not possess and to over-simplify a truly

complex phenomenon. In this respect the insight of the statesman is far more penetrating than the fallacious formulae of historical science. Culture, or civilization, is a living thing. The true significance of a historical event is to be discovered only by the piercing eye of intuition and through a full comprehension of its background. Japan's advance on the continent is partly a racial movement brought about by the operation of Musubi, and only in the light of this fact can Japan's rôle in the China Affair be properly understood and appreciated.

As stated in the Japanese Government's Declaration of January 16, 1938, "Japan expects the establishment and growth of a new Chinese régime with which she will be able to co-operate. And with such a régime she intends to collaborate towards the construction of a newly rehabilitated China." Japan has no intention of demanding abject submission from China. For the purpose of rehabilitating the country she is eager to join forces with China and to work for the adjustment of Sino-Japanese relations on a basis of equality, mutual respect and reciprocity. To conform to the Asiatic ideal and to let Japan and China each manifest and magnify their true individual selves within the Asiatic system—that is, to practise the philosophy of Musubi. Following the dictate of Musubi, Japan, together with a resurrected China, will identify herself with the cosmic force that creates and fosters life and will help to promote its endless process in the beautification and sublimification of Asiatic life. Herein lies the foundation of Japan's China policy.

The Japanese nation is forced to destroy the anti-Japanese régime in China which refuses co-operation and rejects the Asiatic ideal. Deplorable as the present conflict is, it may be made to bear good fruits by those who believe in Musubi. War —the unlimited exercise of brute force — can be made the mother of civilization by those who prac-tise Musubi.

The military operations of Japan are not directed against the peaceful Chinese people. Ours is a campaign for the elimination of the forces of destruction, namely the annihilation of the Kuo-mintang Government and their armies, which, contrary to the Asiatic spirit, obstruct Sino-Japa-nese co-operation.

The warrior of old Japan was brought up

under the moral injunctions of Confucianism and
the spiritual discipline of Buddhism.   The supreme
mission of the warrior was not to fight nor to kill
but "to abstain from violence, to put away arms
and to establish peace."   The true warrior was in
fact not a fighter, but one who identified his military power with the maintenance of peace and the
progressive development of society.   On this point
Bushido coincided with Confucianism which
taught "mastery of self and return to decorum."

The Japanese army is imbued with this ancient spirit of Bushido; it represents "the divine
sword that slays not."   Our forces now fighting
in China are not there merely to kill—but to bring
birth to a new Asia, in which Japan and China,
each maintaining her full independence, will be
merged into one system to create and foster a new
life—a new solidarity of the Asiatic races.

3. THE OBJECTIVE BASIS FOR SINO-JAPANESE CO-OPERATION

The creative aspect of the China Affair cannot be correctly understood save in the light of
the development of Musubi, the life-force of the
Japanese.

In their declaration of January 16 the Japanese
Government frankly and definitely committed
themselves to respect China's sovereignty and territorial integrity and also the rights and interests
of third Powers in China.   Japan, despite her
overwhelming victory won at the sacrifice of many
lives and millions of yen, does not want an inch
of Chinese territory, nor does she entertain any
monopolistic designs there.   This policy of Japan
may seem incomprehensible to Europe which won
its present dominant place in the world through
many series of wars and conquests.   Indeed, the
philosophy of Musubi which underlies Japan's programme of national expansion is entirely alien to
European egoism and the doctrine of opposing
rights and interests.

In the midst of the stupendous tragedy of war
Japan has never lost sight of her constructive goal.
Her policy of non-aggression and non-monopoly
is a concrete embodiment of the Asiatic spirit which
transcends all thought of self.   Let us now examine
the economic basis of the Sino-Japanese co-operation to be fostered by this creative spirit of Asia.

Dr. Sun Yat-sen complains in his book,
"Three People's Principles," of the foreigners

who, regarding the Chinese as incapable of governing their country, have gone even so far as to propose a joint administration of China. "On the other hand," he continues, "Japan in the midst of the storm of Occidental onslaught has successfully built up her national fortune by taking advantage of modern scientific devices, and within fifty years of the opening of the country she has become a great Asiatic Power not to be slighted by any country of Europe or America." Further Dr. Sun remarks: "Japan's rise not only entitles the Yamato race to the honour of being a first-class nation of the world but also enhances the international prestige of Asia as a whole." In this conclusion the Father of the Chinese Revolution frankly admits China's indebtedness to Japan. There is definite proof of the fact that it was due to Japan's rise in power that China was able to ward off European aggression and maintain her independence, even if only in a quasi-colonial fashion. At the same time it may be argued that it was because Japan has not risen sufficiently that China was obliged to become a quasi-colony and an arena to the fierce political and economic contests of Occidental Powers.

The fact that Japan has come to acquire a new position in the world, as is symbolized by the above-mentioned grand rectangular axes overshadowing the North Pacific, is bound to affect the position of quasi-colonial China. Almost simultaneously with the formation of those axes the world became divided into rigid economic units, or blocs, marked off from one another by prohibitive tariff walls. In a world pursuing the doctrine of economic nationalism China can no longer maintain a neutral attitude toward the Powers as in the days of free trade, and will be compelled to pool her economic destiny with one or more Powers.

As Japan became more powerful, the rival Powers of the West found it difficult to establish supremacy over one another in China and to compete successfully with Japan in order to draw China into any one of their orbits. At that moment Chiang Kai-shek and his followers in the Kuomintang party were engaged in building up large armies under the pretext of opposing Japan but in reality for the purpose of strengthening their own position in domestic politics. China's armament expansion provided Occidental nations with a profitable outlet for the products of their heavy industries, and China was obliged to purchase military supplies in ever increasing quantities from Europe and America by reason of her policy of absolute reliance upon the Occidental Powers for the maintenance of her national economy.

Thus China poured forth all her available funds for the purchase of war materials. The financial burden of the Government was shifted onto the shoulders of the largest productive industry of China, namely agriculture, resulting, of course, in the exhaustion of rural communities. Since the market for the products of her textile industry—that had just begun to make headway —lay chiefly in the interior, the impoverishment of the hinterland automatically throttled the new industry. Thus, China plucked off with her own hand the buds of her newly-sprouting industries. There are other factors responsible for the failure of China's programme of economic rehabilitation, but it goes without saying that the greatest blunder was the persistent policy of opposition towards Japan and the adoption of a programme of armament expansion, relying on Europe and America for supplies. Now that the futility of that policy and programme has been demonstrated beyond

the shadow of a doubt, it is time China considered
the Asiatic system of to-morrow and sought a way
for her own salvation.

China's road to salvation lies in the development of her natural resources through Sino-Japanese co-operation.   European and American
nations have ample resources at home or in their
colonies, and they have no need for China's raw
materials.   On the contrary, Japan is in a position
to absorb all China's materials as fast as they are
produced.   Their exploitation may be carried on
under joint investment of Japanese and Chinese
capital.   In addition there is the possibility of par-
ticipation by third countries.   As regards technical
skill and management ability, all requirements can
be readily fulfilled between the two countries.

Japan has already reached a stage of economic
development which obviates all possibility of com-
petition with China.   Japan's shift to heavy industries is expected to prove the propulsive power
to China's light industries, while the development
of Chinese natural resources will accelerate the
progress of Japan's heavy industries.

Sino-Japanese co-operation does not postulate
China's submission to Japan.   In the economic

field as in other fields, co-operation will be realized
upon a footing of equality and reciprocity. China
has drained to the lees the bitter cup of being made
the pawn in the political game of the Powers in
the Far East. Japan has good reason for believing
that with China in such a plight she could not
herself hope to achieve any satisfactory progress,
economic or otherwise.

The economic co-ordination of Japan, Manchoukuo and China as a link in the system of world
economy can alone fulfil the needs of these three
countries and insure the success of the Asiatic
system in which each may develop its resources to
the limits of its ability.

CHAPTER VI

REHABILITATION OF SINO-JAPANESE RELATIONS

1. AFTER A HALF YEAR OF THE CHINA AFFAIR

THE six months subsequent to the Lukou-chiao Incident were marked by a rapid extension of Sino-Japanese hostilities in scope and area. The challenge of China was accepted. The Japanese forces acted swiftly and effectively in North China and in the Yangtze Valley.

With the fall of Nanking the Kuomintang Government, literally broken to pieces, fled to points far in the interior. Even then, Chiang Kai-shek refused to yield. In open alliance with the Communists and aided and abetted by Moscow, Generalissimo Chiang at Hankow continued his futile and desperate "long-time warfare," only to add to the indescribable misery and suffering of China's four hundred millions.

It became evident that Japan now had to take a positive and decisive stand respecting the blind

and inveterate anti-Japanism of the Kuomintang.
On January 11, 1938, an Imperial Conference was
convened, and the following declaration of policy
was issued by the Government under date of January 16:

"Even after the capture of Nanking, the Japanese
Government have till now continued to be patient with a
view to affording a final opportunity for the Chinese National Government to reconsider their attitude. The Chinese Government, however, without appreciating the true
intentions of Japan, blindly persist in their opposition to
this country, with no consideration either internally for the
people in their miserable plight or externally for the peace
and tranquillity of all East Asia. Accordingly, the Japanese Government will cease from henceforward to deal
with that Government, and they look forward to the establishment and growth of a new Chinese régime, with
which harmonious co-ordination can really be counted
upon. With such a régime they will fully co-operate for
the adjustment of Sino-Japanese relations, and for the
building up of a rejuvenated China. Needless to state,
this involves no change in the policy adopted by the Japanese Government of respecting the territorial integrity and
sovereignty of China as well as the rights and interests of
other Powers in China.

"Japan's responsibilities for the peace of East Asia
are now even heavier than ever before.

"It is the fervent hope of the Government that the
people will put forth still greater efforts toward the accom-
plishment of this important task incumbent on the nation."

Thus Japan decided to have no further relations with Chiang Kai-shek. This statement tolled

the death-knell of his régime, the door being definitely closed for negotiations with Tokyo. At the same time, the statement has thrown a ray of hope into the black night of conflict and confusion. It is a beacon-light showing clearly the path Japan is to pursue and heralding the dawn of a new day for East Asia. The statement, moreover, anticipates the emergence of a new Chinese régime, one which is solid, sound and strong, and which is divorced from the anti-Japanese policy of the Kuomintang and dedicated to the cause of Sino-Japanese co-operation and peace. The declaration thus marks a turning point in the history of Sino-Japanese relations from conflict to concord — from destruction to constructive collaboration between Japan and China.

The military operations of the Japanese forces during the past half-year have demonstrated beyond the shadow of a doubt that China is no match for Japan. Neither the crack armies under Chiang's personal command with their modern training and equipment nor the elaborate defence works, upon which Chiang had spent years of work and millions of dollars, and which he boasted to be impregnable, could withstand the onslaught of the

brave and loyal forces of Nippon.   Nanking, de-
fended by a multifold system of modern fortifica-
tions, fell in half a month instead of half a year as
had been anticipated.   No matter where Chiang
may move his capital and military headquarters
and no matter what he may attempt in order to
harass and exhaust Japan, it is now obvious that
he will be completely annihilated.

Chiang Kai-shek and his anti-Japanese clique
were betrayed by over-confidence in their own
ability to fight Japan, and they have learned too
late the folly of flinging down the gauntlet to their
neighbour.   In fact, there were not a few Western
observers who had too highly appraised the fighting strength of Chiang Kai-shek's forces.   They
have now learned that they were wrong.   There
are also a great many foreigners who think it impossible that China and Japan can ever be joined
again on terms of true friendship, but they, too,
will soon discover that they have been wrong.

It is the Kuomintang Government under
Chiang Kai-shek that have inculcated anti-Japanism upon the Chinese mind as a tool of internal
politics for winning popular support and unifying
the country.   Once that government is eliminated

from the picture and that poison expelled from the Chinese body politic, there is bound to arise a new China, and Sino-Japanese co-operation will follow as a natural result. And such co-operation is all that Japan seeks. She does not want to retain an inch of Chinese territory or to impair China's sovereignty. The statement of January 16 is an unequivocal declaration by Japan to all the world of her intention to co-operate with a new China.

The present conflict has awakened in both countries a new moral consciousness as Oriental peoples. It is an enlightenment born of their tragic experience of the past months. They realize the need of restoring peace and order in the Orient on their own responsibility and with their own spiritual resources, casting aside all considerations of material profit. The peace and order of East Asia must be Oriental in structure and principles, and it cannot be realized if the nations are to persist in an egoistic attitude. Japan and China should, by renouncing their individual selves and merging themselves into the common current of East Asia life, strive to create a greater "self."

I am convinced that they are equal to this task by virtue of the noble and splendid spirit of the

East which has been fostered in both countries for centuries past. Both the Japanese and the Chinese peoples have been cast in the same cultural mould. They are spiritual kinsfolk nurtured by Confucianism and Buddhism. They possess the same moral outlook. Cultural similarities are manifested in all phases of their lives. If they reflect a little, coolly and unselfishly, they will find it far easier than expected to arrive at a mutual understanding and to work together for a common cause.

The conclusion arrived at from this half-year of the Sino-Japanese conflict is clearly the necessity of co-operation between Japan and a reborn China.

2. THREE REGIONAL GROUPS FOR WORLD ORDER

The half-year of the China Affair has resulted in the elimination of the Kuomintang Government from the picture. The goal for East Asia in the 20th century is the inauguration of an Asiatic union composed of the Japanese, Chinese, and other Oriental peoples. Japan's statement of January 16, elucidating this point, has already achieved an ideological conquest over the prevailing chaos.

It is to be hoped that Japan and China will not remain for long in a transitional stage of truce,

but that they will set about with a resolute deter-
mination to establish an era of concord and harmony among all Oriental nations.

The civilized world may be divided roughly
into three regional groups—European, American,
and Asiatic. These regions are, it should be noted,
not only distinguishable in point of civilization,
but are also clearly marked off from one another
both historically and geographically.

Upon the conclusion of the Great War the
League of Nations was founded. It seemed then
as though there had come at last a new world
order under one governing body. In the light of
subsequent events, however, it is obvious that mankind has elected to fall into three separate group-
ings, each as a more or less compact and autono-
mous unit.

True, Great Britain, the United States of
America, and Russia are putting forth vigorous
efforts toward the strengthening of their respective
empires. But this is only from the force of man's
conservative habit. The characteristic of this century is the centripetal tendency of all peoples which
causes nations of the world to identify their interests
with those of their respective regional groups.

In 1929 Aristide Briand put forward his plan
for a European Federation.   Europe, he argued,
should not for the sake of its own self-preservation
be torn by contention and rivalry among its individual states, but should join in a federation to
safeguard its civilization and to enhance its prestige and prosperity.   Such was the noble gospel
preached by a statesman who had devoted his whole
life to European politics. Unfortunately, the Briand
plan failed to materialize.   Instead, the European
situation was aggravated by rival alliances, each
seeking to hold the balance of power, and by con-
flicts of interest between individual states.   Nevertheless, the ideal of Briand has caught the imagination of all those statesmen who really desire peace.
And the Pan-European centripetal force has been
seen at work in the conclusion of the New Locarno
Treaty and in the proposal for the reorganization
of the League of Nations.

On the other hand, in the Western hemisphere the Monroe Doctrine, which was rendered
possible largely by geographical factors, has been
steadily evolving into a form of Pan-Americanism.
In December, 1936, the 8th American Conference
was convened at Buenos Aires, which was attended

by the delegates of twenty-one countries. The
Pan-American Union at this conference inaugurated a peace machinery for the Western Hemisphere, which is an epochal achievement in the
history of world politics. The American Secretary
of State, Mr. Cordell Hull, emphasized the need
for the American states to continue to maintain
peaceful and neighbourly relations among themselves in the face of the grave and threatening conditions prevailing elsewhere. He urged that all
unfair discriminatory measures be rejected and the
tariff walls lowered to insure freer trade, so as to
promote the happy position of the new world and
to "let this continent set the high example of
championing the forces of peace, democracy and
civilization."

In the course of some three weeks the Inter-
American Conference reached accord on more
than sixty subjects and drew up a "convention to
co-ordinate, extend and assure the fulfilment of
the existing treaties between American states,"
a "convention for the maintenance, preservation
and re-establishment of peace" and an "additional
protocol relative to non-intervention." The conference adopted a "declaration of principles of

inter-American solidarity and co-operation " and
pledged solemn observance of the doctrine of the
equality, the sovereignty, the territorial integrity
and the liberty of all nations." These agreements
and resolutions, together with a Pan-American international code, the compilation of which had
been previously agreed upon at Montevideo and
Havana, have now perfected an international political organization for the Western Hemisphere.
As is symbolized in the plan for the construction
of a Pan-American Highway, this inter-American
organization promises the moulding of the American republics into one economic unit and the
evolution of fully unified policies respecting tariffs
and currencies. Secretary Hull, who was the
moving spirit of the historic conference, may indeed be said to have blazed a trail for the world
politics of to-morrow.

The inter-American system offers a good concrete example of what is to be expected of a new
world order in which the nations are divided into
three regional groups, self-controlled and self-re-
gulated. Peace and prosperity will surely arrive
in Europe from the adoption of a European system
by European peoples; in America from its self-

controlled inter-Americanism, and in the Orient from the solidarity and harmony of Japan, Manchoukuo and China.

Japan declares unequivocally that she is not thinking of the establishment of Sino-Japanese relations on the basis of victor and vanquished as a reward for her victory in the present war. On the contrary, China and Japan will be put absolutely upon an equal footing. What is desired is an era of great Asiatic concord to be brought about through Japan's collaboration with the new Chinese régime and through the mutual respect of the two nations for each other's sovereignty and territorial integrity.

The New East Asia, as a natural, historic and geographic outgrowth of the Asiatic cultural group, signifies an unfolding of the noble destiny of the Asiatic race. Its development may be viewed as an endless process of growth which enables each Oriental nation to find its own place within the system and to magnify its true individuality while identifying itself with the one great spirit of Asia.

The spirit of the Orient will in its turn become one with the spirit of the world. There is nothing illogical in this. The world spirit exhibits itself partly in the Oriental spirit, and partly in the European spirit and in the American spirit.   And a concrete expression of the Oriental spirit will be seen in the Japanese and Chinese spirits.

Accordingly, the Asiatic system embodying this Oriental spirit carries with it no element of exclusiveness. Japan, occupying the place of leadership, cannot monopolize its advantage, nor can she through selfish motives disregard the rights and interests of third Powers in China, since these constitute a part of that system.

The East Asia of to-morrow is postulated on the real co-operation of Japan and China, based upon equality and mutual respect. The guiding principles of Sino-Japanese relations are "love, benevolence and mutual aid." Admitting of no room for greed or selfishness, they will be governed by the spirit of service and mutual benefit, and the two nations will share equally in the blessings of peace and abundance.

In Europe the forces of destruction operating from the eastern sector will be defeated under the salutary influence of the Berlin-Rome Axis. When Europe agrees upon a policy that will allow virile nations, such as Germany and Italy, access to raw materials and markets and enables them to find adequate financial facilities with a view to safe-guarding and advancing European peace and civil-ization, there is not the slightest doubt as to the early and triumphant inauguration of a European system. The world will rest secure on the tripod of these politico-cultural regional groups in America, Europe and Asia, each group endeavouring to promote peace and economic welfare in its own sphere and develop its own peculiar civilization and culture. And then, when mutual and co-operative relations are cultivated among these three groups, we may hope to banish in the end the tragedy of war from the face of the earth. The tripartite division of the world is thus only an antecedent to the unitary evolution and progress of mankind.

3. POLITICAL UNIFICATION OF JAPAN, MANCHOUKUO AND CHINA

The present-day world is, as has been noted, tending to fall into three politico-cultural divisions. A new Asiatic system of harmony is about to emerge from extreme discord and chaos, as Japan and China, the two great nations of the Asiatic area, discover the key to unity and co-operation through the terrible holocaust of the present war.

The declaration of the Japanese Goverment of January 16 this year, which sets forth a determined stand against Chiang Kai-shek, heralds the birth of a new order in Asia. It is based on what is called *jen* in Confucianism, which means perfect virtue or humanity and requires one not only to love the good but to hate the bad and to punish the wicked. It is the spirit of *jen* that compels Japan to reject and destroy the unethical Kuomintang régime.

This Asiatic system, being a historical and cultural product indigenous to the soil, is to be regulated by the moral traditions of Asia. It would be absolutely impossible to adjust satisfactorily the many difficulties between Japan and China merely by focussing our attention upon the political and economic factors alone. We should begin first by clarifying the questions regarding the guiding spirit and the world outlook that are needed for a fundamental solution. Then will be laid the cornerstone for the construction of a new Asiatic system. Let the nations of East Asia—Japan, Manchoukuo and China—casting aside all materialistic and selfish considerations, join in the true spirit of Asia.

Let the three nations stand as one in virtue and prepare for the rôle they are to play in the history of the world.

The realization of the "Three nations, one in virtue" will lead inevitably to their political unification. This political unification, however, does not involve absorption or annexation. Nor is it to rest upon a relationship between conqueror and conquered. It means a federation of independent states for a common ideal — a combination calculated to promote individual development as well as the harmony of the whole. In order to maintain peace and order in East Asia and to further the happiness and welfare of its peoples, Japan, Manchoukuo and China with a common world outlook are to co-operate in the neighbourly spirit of amity, goodwill and mutual helpfulness. Above all, there must be mutual confidence. In the Confucian Analeçts we find the following dialogue between the Chinese sage and one of his disciples:

Tsu-kung asked about government. The Master said there should be sufficiency of food, sufficiency of arms and the confidence of the people in their government.

Tsu-kung said, "If it cannot be helped and one of these three must be dispensed with, which one should go?"

"Let go the arms," said the Master.

Tsu-kung said, "If it cannot be helped and one of
these two must be dispensed with, which one should go?"
"Let go the food," said the Master. "From of old,
death has been the lot of all men. Without the people's
confidence the government will not stand."

Japan, Manchoukuo and China "will not
stand" if mutual confidence is lacking. The basis
of the Asiatic system should not be armed force
but mutual confidence which may well be embodied in an "Inter-Asiatic Code" to be compiled
as a political instrument.

In the first century of the Christian era the
Hans built a world empire and created a system
of law and education in order to rule the alien
races inhabiting their wide domain. To-day the
nations of Asia should strive for the creation of a
federation of fraternal states, founded upon equality
and mutual respect, and aiming at the preservation
of the full sovereignty and independence of its respective members.

The British Empire offers an example of such
a federation of independent nations, skilfully and
elaborately organized for the advancement of their
common interests, while in the American con-
tinents the centripetal unification movement is conspicuously at work against the centrifugal forces of

the colonial days that gave birth to the present republics. As mankind has reached its present stage
of development, the existing world order is absolutely inadequate to meet the cultural and economic necessities of nations.   The division of the
world into three regional groups is but a natural
development in the twentieth century.   The unification for common defence and development of
kindred races and of areas having the same culture
and civilization constitutes the vital problem that
confronts us to-day.

    . The Sino-Japanese conflict will prove an in-
finite blessing when it ends in the establishment
of the Asiatic system and the achievement of political unification, known as "Tatung" (great oneness) in China and "Daiwa" (great harmony) in
Japan. This will be a momentous step toward the
realization of the ideal of "The world, one household."

4. ECONOMIC UNIFICATION OF JAPAN, MANCHOUKUO AND CHINA

    The important aspects of the civilization of
Asia are mostly confined to the spiritual field, while
European civilization is more conspicuously mark-

ed by scientific and material progress. The decline of the Asiatic peoples in the modern age is due to the fact that they have neglected science and have ignored the laws of nature as well as the political, social and economic laws of man; and that they have forgotten how important and how sacred is mundane life. The Asiatic peoples, while preparing to build an Asiatic system on the basis of their profound spiritual enlightenment, should examine the history of the economic and political achievements of Europe in order to formulate a more effective means of realizing their lofty ideals.

As has already been pointed out, at the present stage of human progress no country can fully satisfy its multifarious needs by the resources to be found within its own boundaries, but it must inevitably seek to expand its sphere of cultural and economic activity. Japan, Manchoukuo and China, fully appreciating the world significance of the motto, "Three nations, one in virtue," and their relationship of mutuality, should co-operate for their common prosperity under the Asiatic system so as to make their countries a powerful link in the future chain of world economy.

The Japan-Manchoukuo Protocol which was

signed immediately after the establishment of Manchoukuo and all the subsequent treaties are intended for the co-ordination of the economies of
the two neighbour nations. It will naturally be
extended to embrace China. Because Japan was
able to establish securely an inseparable relationship with Manchoukuo, she has been able to
strengthen enormously the position of the two
nations *vis-à-vis* other Powers. The recent extension of economic imperialism everywhere has done
much to paralyze world economy, so that in the
face of this actual trend Japan has been compelled
to expand her own economic sphere. On the
other hand, with the collapse of the world's economic structure built upon free trade, China, as a
quasi-colony maintained by the balance of power
among the stronger nations, began to lose rapidly
the basis of her independence. England and
America, which had perfected their respective
systems of *bloc* economy, regarded China only as a
market for their commodities. They had more
raw material than they could use; and they were
in no need of China's agricultural or mineral products. Japan, with her heavy industries rapidly expanding in the wake of the Manchurian Incident,

was in a position to help China's economic reconstruction by absorbing Chinese products.   Viewed
objectively, Japan with her heavy industries and
China with her growing light industries were in
an ideal position for mutually profitable trade and
economic co-operation.

China could have found no better chance for
economic reconstruction and development than
by collaborating with Japan.   Nevertheless, the
Chinese Government disregarded the realities of
the situation and continued to rely more and more
on Britain and America.   But these Occidental
Powers confined their economic operations in
China to selling ammunition and rolling stock,
constructing military railways and highways and
reforming the currency system in order to facilitate
the sale of their goods. The opening up of China's
natural resources was largely neglected, with the
result that China's basic economy was seriously
atrophied.

The weakness of the Chinese economic structure was exposed as soon as the present hostilities
broke out, since it rested almost entirely on British
and American support.   In modern warfare the
contending Powers must match all their national

resources, industrial and otherwise, and in such a war the huge Chinese army is of little use. This disastrous conflict is, however, by the curious irony of fate, paving the way to the establishment of the Asiatic system so that a tripartite economic alliance between Japan, Manchoukuo and China is now expected in a not distant future.

Economic development depends much on the progress of science. China, despite her early contact with European civilization, has remained impervious to its scientific influence, lagging far behind Japan in this respect. China's eyes have been opened by the scientific development which has taken place in the Island Empire. This one fact alone is sufficient to confirm historically the Chinese need for economic and technical co-operation with Japan. When a good specimen of American cotton was transplanted in Shantung, the stock rapidly degenerated in a few years. But the same cotton, first planted and acclimatized in Chosen, proved capable of thriving in Shantung, so that now a considerable amount of good cotton is produced yearly in that Chinese province. This is but a casual instance of the happy result of Japanese technical assistance to Chinese agriculture.

It should be stressed that equality and mutual respect must govern the economic as well as the political relations of China and Japan under the Asiatic system. The advent of *bloc* economy in the world provides China with a Heaven-sent opportunity to throw off her quasi-colonial status, while her entry into the Asiatic system will assure her political and economic independence. When Japan, Manchoukuo and China are welded into a rational and organic economic unit, the Asiatic system will operate most effectively and its potential powers will be brought into full play.

Under this system a peaceful and orderly China, with her vast territory and well-nigh inexhaustible man-power, and Japan, with her industrial experience and ability and technical skill, can join forces in exploiting the rich natural resources of the Asiatic mainland. Among the principal products of China are iron, salt, cotton, wheat and wool. The British Empire and America are amply supplied with these products within their own territories, and it can hardly be expected that they will undertake to tap China's resources which would only flood their own markets. The natural outlet for the raw materials produced in China is

Japan, her next-door neighbour, who will buy them in exchange for the manufactured articles turned out by Japanese industries. The unification of the complementary economies of Japan and China will provide mutual benefits and prosperity and will create an excellent example of international co-operation for those nations whose trade channels are at present intolerably encumbered under the existing system of prohibitive tariffs and discriminatory restrictions. A concrete programme of economic unification might begin with such fundamental steps as the opening of airways, the unification of railway services and the conclusion of tariff treaties on the basis of reciprocity.

5. UNIFICATION OF LANGUAGE

Intellectual co-operation under the Asiatic system appears to be a comparatively easy matter. This is fortunate and brightens the prospects of the Asiatic system, for cultural co-operation in all fields constitutes the basic condition of international peace.

Japan, Manchoukuo and China have the same cultural foundation and they possess a common system of writing. Japan's contact with China

dates far back into the legendary age.   But her
actual cultural intercourse with the Asiatic continent may be considered to have commenced with
the conquest of Korea by the Empress Jingu early
in the 3rd century.   It is recorded that in the reign
of the Emperor Ojin, son of the Empress Jingu,
Chinese classics were presented to the court, and
Prince Wakairatsuko of Uji had for his tutor a
naturalized Korean known by the name of Achiki.

Subsequently Japan imported with astounding
speed and thoroughness Chinese arts and crafts—
and most important of all, Chinese ideographs and
literature.   To be sure the Japanese did not aban-
don their own language, which in origin and
structure is totally different from Chinese.   They
adopted the Chinese ideographs for their own pur-
poses, sometimes as words in their original sense
and sometimes as phonetic symbols for transcribing
Japanese words for which there were no Chinese
equivalents.   Nevertheless, they studied the Chinese classics and learned to write prose and poetry
in pure Chinese.   In fact, for many centuries Chinese remained the official language of the court
and the élite, as far as written compositions were
concerned.   It occupied in Japan a place some-

what analogous to that of Latin in medieval Europe. In the 8th century Prince Shotoku, the famous patron of Buddhism, wrote in erudite and elegant Chinese the *Sankyo Giso*, commentaries on three Buddhist sutras which were then current in Japan. An interesting fact is that the first book begins with the line reading: "These are the personal work of the High Imperial Prince of Japan; they are not books from beyond the sea." In fact they contained interpretations and opinions of the Prince adopted from an independent Japanese standpoint. Copies of these books were taken back by a Chinese priest to his homeland and presented to a great monastery in the city of Yang-chow.

Abe Nakamaro, a student sent to China during the Tang period, was so captivated by the brilliance of the Chinese capital that he chose to remain there. He was appointed to a post at the court of the Emperor Hsuan-tsung, was promoted to a higher post in the reign of the next Emperor and died in China.

These episodes, though fragmentary, give evidence of the free and friendly intercourse which existed in those days between China and Japan.

They indicate that the two countries were not only joined by one cultural stream flowing from China to Japan, but that there was another stream flowing back from Japan to China.

With the coming of the Meiji Restoration in 1867, Japan, by absorbing and assimilating Occidental civilization with her characteristic diligence and skill, quickly superseded China in scientific progress. Japan invented a host of words compounded of old Chinese ideographs but signifying things entirely new—namely, the terminologies of Western science and philosophy. And these new words were taken back home by Chinese students, presenting the curious spectacle of old Chinese ideographs, laden with new meanings, flowing in copious streams back to China from Japan. Through the medium of the Chinese ideograph, the Japanese and Chinese have long forged an indestructible bond of moral and spiritual kinship. Now thanks to the same medium, the two nations have a large stock of common terminologies of the modern age.

There exists, of course, a divergency between Japan and China in the pronunciation of many ideographs, and there are a number of compounds which mean one thing in Japan and quite another thing in China.   Finally, there is the fundamental and structual difference between the Japanese and Chinese languages.   It may be too much to expect the possibility of creating one common spoken language for Japan, Manchoukuo and China, but at the same time, it should not be difficult to organize a language alliance under competent leadership for the adjustment of certain types of vocabulary to a degree sufficient to simplify ordinary social intercourse and commercial transactions among the three nations.   And in time we may hope to have a complete linguistic unification so as to enable the three nations to live in an identical world of thought and speech.

CHAPTER VII

CONCLUSION

DAWN OF A NEW ASIA

THAT the Sino-Japanese problem should have been thrown into the maelstrom of armed conflict is a most deplorable and shameful thing for Asia. It is an indelible blot on the history of the Asiatic race.

Nevertheless, if the China Affair has brought a black night upon Asia, the dawn of a new era is not far ahead. In North China and the Yangtze Valley, wherever the Sun flag waves side by side with the five-coloured flag, we see already signs of a new order for which the Japanese Government's statement of January 16 is a solemn pledge. The longer the Kuomintang Government persist in their avowed opposition, the wider will be extended the territories over which shall wave the Rising Sun and the old emblem of the Chinese Republic. It may be that the pitiable and stubborn manœu-vres of Chiang Kai-shek are nothing but a neces-

sary step towards the consolidation of Asia—a sort
of churning process that is to bring about a new
and more solid Asiatic unity.

At any rate, for this catastrophic development
of Sino-Japanese relations, Japan is not entirely free
of blame.   Seeing which way the Kuomintang
Government was drifting in the turbulent waters
of China's internal politics, she could have acted,
perhaps, in time to prevent Chiang Kai-shek from
dragging her into the abyss.   For this failure on
her part, Japan owes an apology to mankind, but
at the same time she is obliged to wield her sword
to remove all the forces of treachery, iniquity and
ruthless destruction.

The Kuomintang Government have feverishly
and frantically resorted to every possible device to
enlist outside assistance and to invite the interven-
tion of third Powers in a war which they themselves had started.   The machinery of the League
of Nations was set in motion.   The Nine Power
Treaty was invoked.   The representatives of the
European Powers interested in preserving a quasi-
colonial China were readily led by false propaganda
into outbursts of sentimentalism.   They failed
utterly to take a long view of things, in the in-

terests of the real peace and tranquillity of Asia and
the common welfare of mankind.   Is it that a
cultural unification or fusion is impossible of attainment without war?   "Heaven lies," said Moham-
med, "in the shadow of the sword."   It is the
irony of fate that Japan's quest for peaceful co-
operation should have ended in open hostilities.
It is to be hoped that the present affair shall not
prove to be only one scene in a still more terrible
tragedy—the conflict of the East and West with
China as the stage.

The Anglo-Saxons with their admirable prac-
tical spirit may view the China Affair as an inevitable outcome of Japan's expansion, which is bound
to monopolize the field to the exclusion of their
own interests.   Indeed, the Japan Axes, repre-
senting the growth of the nation in the northern
Pacific, does, Proteus-like, assume varied forms in
the imagination of different observers.

Japan's position as the stabilizing force in East
Asia carries in itself a mission of historical significance which must cause the natural extinction of
the Nine Power Treaty.   In other words, between
1922, when that treaty was concluded, and to-day,
when Japan's axes have been completed, there

have occurred drastic changes the world over, and it is not possible to settle any Asiatic problem without recognizing Japan's new position in the northern Pacific. The axes of new Japan symbolize a moral obligation not to leave China a prize for endless international rivalries but to rescue her from the state of a quasi-colony of Occidental Powers. Asia should realize to its noble obligation to promote its unique and sublime spiritual life and to contribute to the advancement of mankind through free and whole-hearted co-operation with the rest of the world. The spirit of Asia awoke from its long sleep of centuries first in Japan through contact with Western civilization. The emergence of Japan as a new living force marked only the opening page of the history of the Asiatic race. With the China Affair begins its main chapter.

Thus, the military operations that Japan was compelled to take in China should be looked upon as a manifestation of the creative power of the Asiatic spirit, from which we may well expect the consummation of a constructive peace. The China Affair, which has rudely shaken the world, is destined to prove the very centre of the stream in the swift current of world history.

The Brussels Conference, which was summoned for the purpose of settling the Sino-Japanese conflict, served as an antidote against the poison of European imperialism which has paralyzed China since the time of the Opium War. It is time the Nine Power Treaty was re-examined and diagnosed to clarify its basic pollution.

The Asiatic peoples should cast aside all the selfish individualism and materialism of Europe. They should embrace one common faith of Asia and live an Asiatic life. The Confucianism that originated in China and was perfected in Japan, as if anticipating the needs of to-day, long ago laid down the stern and solemn code of " self-mastery and return to decorum." Herein lies the common ideal for Japan, Manchoukuo and China.

Through the mastery of self and the purification of group life, all the nations of Asia may be united in the Asiatic spirit and under Asiatic order and discipline, while retaining fully individual independence and mutual respect among themselves.

The search for *Zipangu*, the Eldorado of Marco Polo, led to the discovery of the American Continent. And it was the United States that, rising on that new continent, forced open the door of the hermit nation, Japan. Now it is Japan's turn to arouse her neighbour country to the west from its lethargic sleep of centuries. *Lux ex oriente*. Japan is the pioneer of a new age; she is the hope of a new Asia.

THE END

INDEX

115

perialism, 57; "Japanese imperialism," 63

Industrial output ; — of the world, 24;—of Japan, 22-23

Inoue, Dr. Tetsujiro, 46

Inter-American Conference, 89, 90

Inter-Asiatic Code, 97

Ishiwara, Dr. Jun, 42

Italy, 11, 12, 13, 93

Iyasaka (Prosper ever!), 70

Jaluit Island, 32, 33, 34

Japan; economic power, 21-25, 64; education, 25-27; national defence, 27, 29-31; spiritual development, 35-39; statistics of foreign trade, 52, 53; shipping industry, 53; capital on Asiatic continent, 54; emigration, 55; factors of expansion, 64; China policy, 74; early contact with China, 104-106.

Japan-Manchoukuo Protocol, 33, 99

"Jen," 95

Jimmu, Emperor, 35

Jingu, Empress, 56, 105

Jodo-shu, 38

Kakeya, Dr. Soichi, 41

Kamakura Period, 38

Kant, 49

Kasho Island, 32

Kikuchi, Dr. Dairoku, 41

Kimmei, Emperor, 37

Kitazato Institute, 43

Kobo Daishi, 38

Konjiki-in, 71

Korea, see Chosen

Kropotkin, 48

K. S. steel, 43

Kublai Khan, 56, 59

Kumaso, the, 56

Kuomintang Government, 10, 68, 74, 82, 83, 85, 87, 95, 109, 110; Party, 78, 84

Lancashire, 54

Language unification between Japan, Manchoukuo and China, 104

League of Nations, 11, 14, 28, 88, 89, 110

Leibnitz, 40

Liao dynasty, 58

"Liberty," 13

"long-time warfare," 82

Lukouchiao Incident, 82

Malay Peninsula, 51; Malay race, 69

Manchoukuo, 16, 17, 33, 51, 54, 58, 60, 65, 81, 92, 94, 95, 96, 97, 98, 99, 100, 104, 108, 113

Manchouli, 33, 34

Manchurian Incident, 10, 22, 23, 28, 34, 47, 48, 53, 57, 100